Wedding Attendants

Selecting & Directing
Your Supporting Cast

WEDDING ATTENDANTS

Selecting &
Directing
Your
Supporting
Cast

JO PACKHAM

A Sterling/Chapelle Book
Sterling Publishing Co., Inc. New York

Jo Packham
Author

Tina Annette Brady
Designer

Cherie Hanson
Editor

Margaret Shields Marti
Executive Editor

Library of Congress Cataloging-in-Publication Data

Packham, Jo.
    Wedding attendants : selecting & directing your supporting cast /
by Jo Packham.
        p.   cm.
    "A Sterling/Chapelle book."
    Includes index.
    ISBN 0-8069-8829-0
    1. Wedding attendants.   I. Title.
    BJ2065.W43P33   1993   93-14159
    395V' .22--dc20   CIP

10 9 8 7 6 5 4 3 2 1

A Sterling/Chapelle Book

Published by Sterling Publishing Company, Inc.
387 Park Avenue South, New York, N.Y. 10016
© 1993 by Chapelle Ltd.
Distributed in Canada by Sterling Publishing
$^{c}/_{o}$ Canadian Manda Group, P.O. Box 920, Station U
Toronto, Ontario, Canada M8Z 5P9
Distributed in Great Britain and Europe by Cassell PLC
Villiers House, 41/47 Strand, London WC2N 5JE, England
Distributed in Australia by Capricorn Link Ltd.
P.O. Box 665, Lane Cove, NSW 2066
Manufactured in the United States of America

Sterling ISBN 0-8069-8829-0

Contents

> *Friends cherish each other's hopes.*
> *They are kind to each other's dreams.*
>
> Henry David Thoreau

Making and enjoying memories is one of the treasures you share with friends. That is why the selection of who is to be in your wedding with you and your fiancé is such an important part of one of the most meaningful events of both of your lives.

Your Supporting Cast

Asking someone to be a wedding participant is not only an ancient custom but an honor and a great responsibility. In the past, there were definite rules about whom should be included, absolute guidelines on what their roles should be, and every member of the wedding party had a well-defined area of responsibility. Today, however, with modern mobility, career obligations, and scattered families, you and your fiancé will have to decide what is best for the two of you, your families, and your wedding participants. Perhaps it would be easiest to begin with the traditional guidelines and then rewrite them to suit your own personal wants and needs. If it works for the two of you and it does not intentionally offend anyone else, then consider it appropriate!

You will want to include both family and friends in your wedding party, and you will want to make the selections with great care so as not to hurt anyone's feelings. It is a very nice gesture if you each ask a few members of the other's family to join your wedding party even though you or your fiancé may not know the person to be included as well as other members you have selected. You might ask the groom's sister to be your bridesmaid, and the groom might ask your brother to be a groomsman.

Neither of you ever need to feel obligated to include someone in your wedding party simply because you were part of theirs nor do the two of you need to feel obligated for any other reasons. You can "what if" yourselves forever and worry about everyone because there will always be someone that you "probably should" ask to participate. In reality, what you both need is to do what you feel is right in your hearts and be honest with everybody, those who are involved as well as those the two of you have elected not to involve. You can always invite those who are not to be in the wedding party to participate in one of the different ways described later; see page 52.

Contact all wedding party members and ask them to participate immediately after the engagement is announced and contact all of them as close to the same time as possible. The invitation to participate should be issued in person or, if they live a great distance, by telephone or in a letter. No one should refuse the honor of being in the wedding party unless it is absolutely impossible. If one of the wedding party is forced to withdraw unexpectedly, you may leave the position vacant or, even up to the last day or two, ask another close friend or relative to take the absent person's place. Friends or family members should not be offended by such a late invitation, but rather should be flattered that you feel close enough to count on them in an emergency.

Remember that not everyone is aware of his or her responsibilities— especially if they are young or have never participated in a wedding before. Do not assume that they know what is expected of them and do not hesitate to talk to them about their duties, responsibilities, and your expectations. Never expect more of your wedding party than they can reasonably afford to give—both in time and financial considerations. You want your wedding to be as memorable for your participants as you do for you and the groom.

Two of the features of this book are the thorough, easy-to-use lists of responsibilities for individuals of your wedding party and the checklists. You will want to review all the possibilities and, with your intended, itemize particular information on each person's worksheet. Give him or her a copy and keep one for yourself. Of course, accompanying the worksheet with a handwritten note makes the wedding "business" seem more personal.

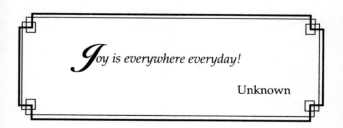

Joy is everywhere everyday!

Unknown

Wedding Party Timetable

❦ Six to twelve months before the wedding

1. Select and invite wedding party and participants.

2. Select and order maid/matron-of-honor's, attendants', and other female participants' attire and accessories.

3. Select and order best man's, ushers', and other male participants' attire and accessories.

4. Make initial reservations for bridal party accommodations.

❦ Three months before the wedding

1. Schedule bridesmaids' and female participants' dress and shoe fittings.

2. Schedule maid/matron-of-honor (and bridesmaids, if necessary) to help address all wedding invitations.

❧ *Two months before the wedding*

1. Mail invitations.

2. Finalize and confirm accommodations and reservations for bridal party.

❧ *One month before the wedding*

1. Purchase gifts for bridal party.

2. Schedule final fittings, including accessories and shoes for maid/matron-of-honor, bridesmaids, and other female participants and for best man, groomsmen, and other male participants.

3. Schedule appointments at beauty salon for attendants.

4. Make the arrangements for a place for your bridesmaids to dress before the ceremony and notify the bridesmaids.

5. Send invitations to your wedding party, notifying them of the time and place of the rehearsal and rehearsal dinner.

6. Prepare and deliver individual responsibility checklists to participants, helpers and others.

❧ *One week before the wedding*

Arrange for one last fitting of all wedding attire for all wedding party members and participants.

❧ *Your wedding day*

1. Have maid/matron-of-honor arrive at your home two hours before the ceremony to help you begin dressing. You may wish to have your mother assist.

2. Have attendants arrive at a prearranged place. If it is someplace where all attendants will dress together, they should arrive two hours before the ceremony. If everyone is scheduled to meet at the ceremony site already dressed, they should arrive one hour early.

3. Ten minutes before the ceremony is to begin all attendants take their places to begin the processional.

The Honor Attendant

The honor attendant is one of the most important roles in the wedding. She will help you in every way needed during the preparations for the wedding and throughout the actual festivities. You will need to select that perfect someone whom you are closer to than any other and someone you can depend upon and trust to be responsible and diligent in her duties. She will be the one who thinks of the things you forget and who is there to keep you calm, offering support in a time that is filled with excitement, decision making, and, always, just a hint of doubt.

The maid/matron (if she is married)-of-honor traditionally is a sister, a family member, or a very close friend who is approximately your age. In the case of a second marriage, she may be a daughter or stepdaughter. If she is very young, she becomes the maiden-of-honor. It is becoming very acceptable to select your mother, grandmother or other favorite older relative to be your honor attendant. In your mother's case, be careful not to ask too much of her because she is still the official hostess of the wedding festivities and her duties are many. In some contemporary wedding parties, an honor attendant is chosen who may be a person such as a brother, male cousin or other male friend or relative who is very close to you.

Traditionally, only one person is selected to be a maid- or matron-of-honor but you may elect to have two. You may have a family member or friend who is your age or older and is married and she becomes your matron-of-honor, while another friend or family member who may be younger and single becomes your maid-of-honor. If you select two honor attendants, some etiquette books say that the "maid" takes precedence, holding the bouquet and serving as a witness. On the other hand, you may choose to have the older of the two take the majority of the responsibility (in respect for her age and because she may be capable of helping you more). Another choice is to have them split the duties equally. For example, one could hold your bouquet during the ceremony while one hands you the groom's ring. If you select two honor attendants, the younger of the two could go first in the processional with the older being the one directly preceding the flower girl, or they could walk side by side down the aisle, or they could reverse roles in the processional and recessional. The same order should be observed in the receiving line and at the table during the dinner that was observed during the processional.

Responsibilities

1. The honor attendant assists in making all of the arrangements; reminds you of details; offers support; and in general, works to make the entire wedding process as problem free as possible.

2. She usually pays for her own wedding attire and all accessories, except for her flowers, as well as her own travel expenses (except for her hotel accommodations which should be paid by you).

3. She will help you with any pre-wedding duties such as addressing envelopes for the ceremony and reception. She may also help you with the shopping or the coordinating of special events.

4. She supervises the bridesmaids and the flower girl. She makes certain their dresses are fitted or purchased, that they have all of the accessories they will need, that they perform all of their responsibilities, and that they get to the wedding rehearsal and ceremony on time.

5. She attends all pre-wedding parties and showers she is invited to and perhaps hosts one herself. You should make certain that she understands that you do not expect her to give a gift at every shower. One gift in addition to her wedding gift, regardless of how many showers or parties she attends, is all that is necessary. If, because of expenses such as travel and wedding attire, it is going to be a considerable expense for your honor attendant, you may wish to make it clear to her that no gifts are expected at all—her presence and help are presents enough.

6. She records the giver and gift at all gift openings.

7. She attends the rehearsal and rehearsal dinner.

8. She helps you dress the morning of the wedding and accompanies you to the church (unless you arrive formally in a limousine with your father).

9. At a home wedding, she is the one who is responsible for greeting the ceremony official and showing him or her where to change clothes.

10. The honor attendant signs the marriage certificate as a witness if she is 18 years or older (which is the required age for signing a legal document). If she is not old enough, your mother or an older bridesmaid could sign the document.

11. She follows the bridesmaids and precedes the flower girl down the aisle.

12. She arranges your train and veil (if your wedding is a formal one) at the beginning and during the ceremony and holds your bouquet during the exchanging of rings.

13. She holds the groom's ring and passes it to you at the appropriate time, if there is no ring bearer. During the ceremony she may elect to wear the ring on her middle finger or thumb, carry it in a hidden pocket, or place it in a dainty bag that she carries in conjunction with her flowers.

14. She helps in coordinating all of the bridesmaids so everyone is available for formal picture taking before and after the ceremony and during the reception.

15. Traditionally, she stands next to the groom on his left in the receiving line, but it is becoming customary in some parts of the country for her to stand on your right. She will take the same place, on the groom's left, if there is formal seating at a dinner during the reception.

16. She dances with the groom (after you, the groom's mother, and your mother have had their turn), then with both fathers, best man, and other male attendants.

17. She helps you change out of your wedding gown and into your going-away clothes at the end of the reception.

18. She makes certain none of your belongings are left at the church or she arranges to have someone handle this responsibility for her.

19. She is the one who makes certain that your wedding gown is put in safe keeping until your return from your honeymoon. She will also make certain that your bouquet is either refrigerated until your return or given to the florist for preservation.

20. She should be the one you ask to help with details that need to be attended to while you are honeymooning. She can deposit checks, transport presents or help to make certain that thank-you flowers are sent to both your and the groom's parents.

Checklist for Honor Attendant

Maid/Matron-of-Honor_____

Phone_____

Address_____

Travel Arrangements_____

Accommodations_____

Special Duties_____

_____

_____

_____

_____

_____

_____

_____

_____

_____

_____

_____

The Best Man

The best man was historically the groom's brother or closest friend. Today, especially if this is the groom's second marriage, he may choose his father, grandfather, or son. Next to you and the groom, the best man shares with your honor attendant the distinction of being the most important member of the wedding party. He is the one who will help the groom with some of the decision making; he is the one who is always there to bolster the groom's confidence; and he is the one to supply reassurance and support. His duties are many and his responsibilities important for he is to relieve the groom of as many details and as much responsibility as possible. If there is no wedding coordinator, the best man, the maid/matron-of-honor, and the wedding hosts are responsible for making certain that the ceremony and reception go exactly as planned. He is the one who should be prepared for and handle any emergency! He, therefore, should be the friend or relative the groom selects over any other, not only because he is the closest but because he is the most responsible, dependable, and has the best sense of humor!

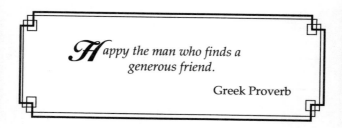

Happy the man who finds a generous friend.

Greek Proverb

Responsibilities

1. The best man will assist the groom with any necessary arrangements.

2. He usually pays for or rents his own wedding attire and accessories (except for his neckwear, gloves, and boutonniere) as well as his own travel expenses (except for his hotel accommodations which should be paid by the groom).

3. He attends all pre-wedding festivities that he is invited to, the rehearsal and rehearsal dinner.

4. Some time before the wedding, either with the ushers or with their approval, he selects the gift that they will present the groom. He is responsible for all details of the gift: collecting the money, making certain it is engraved or printed, and presenting it to the groom on everyone's behalf (usually at the rehearsal dinner or the bachelor party/dinner).

5. He makes certain the groom's formal attire is picked up before the wedding.

6. He helps the groom pack for his honeymoon and double-checks all of the details—money or traveler's checks, passports, car keys, transportation tickets, hotel reservations, and so on. He also makes certain the clothes the groom will wear when he leaves the reception are packed in a different bag. He then delivers both bags to the reception site.

7. He organizes and hosts the bachelor party or dinner.

8. He makes certain the groom is dressed in plenty of time and he drives the groom to the wedding ceremony.

9. He makes certain that the ushers are on time, properly dressed, and briefed again about the ceremony procedures and their responsibilities.

10. He holds the ring to be given to the bride until it is time to exchange rings during the ceremony unless the ring bearer is doing so.

11. He enters the church immediately after the groom and stands next to the groom during the ceremony.

12. He escorts the maid/matron-of-honor down the aisle during the recessional.

13. Immediately following the recessional or receiving line, he sees both you and the groom to the waiting car. In the absence of a chauffeur, he is the one who drives you to the reception site.

14. The best man is in charge of and signs the marriage certificate as a witness if he is 18 years or older (which is the required age for signing a legal document). If he is not old enough, the groom's father or an older usher may sign the document.

15. He makes certain to get all payment checks from the groom or the groom's father and then gives one payment check to the officiant either just before or immediately after the ceremony. He disperses similar checks to service providers as needed. (Certainly, some of these checks may have to be obtained from the bride's family).

16. Along with the official wedding hosts, he attends to any emergencies that might arise during the ceremony or reception.

17. He helps to gather the groomsmen together for all formal picture taking before and after the ceremony and during the reception.

18. If you choose to have him do so, he stands in the receiving line; otherwise, he mingles with the guests and sees to his other responsibilities. If there is a bridal dinner, he sits on your right.

19. It is his responsibility to make the first toast to you and the groom and to announce or introduce family members. He will also read any telegrams or messages that have arrived. (He keeps the telegrams for safe keeping and delivers them to your parents immediately after the reception or to you on your return from your honeymoon.)

20. He is the first man to dance with you after the groom, your father-in-law, and your father. He then dances with both mothers, the maid/matron-of-honor, and other female attendants.

21. Immediately before you choose to leave the reception, he is responsible for escorting both families to the dressing rooms for their farewells. He will then lead the two of you through the waiting guests to the door.

22. He is in charge of the transportation you will use to leave the reception, and he keeps these plans secret and the car hidden so as to avoid any practical jokes. He makes certain your and your groom's luggage are in the car. Then, he is personally responsible to drive the two of you to the hidden automobile or makes the arrangements to have the car delivered immediately before your departure.

23. He makes certain to return the groom's attire (if it was rented) or keeps the groom's personally owned attire until he returns from the honeymoon.

24. He arranges to have flowers or a bottle of chilled champagne delivered to your hotel room just before your arrival.

25. He organizes the return of all groomsmen's rented formal wear, deposits money gifts into appropriate accounts and can work with the honor attendant to make certain all gifts are delivered to a predetermined location.

Checklist for the Best Man

Best Man_____

Phone_____

Address_____

Travel Arrangements_____

Accommodations_____

Special Duties_____

_____

_____

_____

_____

_____

_____

_____

_____

_____

_____

_____

> *A joy that is shared is a joy made whole.*
>
> English proverb

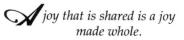

Wedding Attendants

You have decided to marry, discussed and established a budget, chosen a wedding style and selected your honor attendant and best man. Now the two of you should think about how many attendants each of you will have and who they will be.

You will need to be selective, consider the feelings of family and friends, begin with traditional guidelines, and then modify them to fit your own personal needs.

Bridesmaids

Historically, bridesmaids were literally unmarried "maids." Today, you are free to choose any family member or friend who is close to you and who you sincerely want to share one of the most important times of your life. Remember, however, that it is a nice gesture on your part to ask at least one relative of the groom to be in your bridal party, even if you barely know him or her or have never met them. If there are more special friends than places in the wedding party, include those who are not selected to be bridesmaids to be honored in a different way. They may read a scripture or poem during the ceremony or you may offer them a special toast during the reception.

Traditionally, twelve bridesmaids was the limit regardless of how formal the wedding. Today, however, you may have as many as the occasion warrants and you can afford. The number may be even or uneven, it may be the same number as the groomsmen (which was historically calculated at one groomsman for every 50 guests) or it may be different, as long as it is not too imbalanced. At the wedding rehearsal you can find a variety of ways to create an attractive procession and recession, regardless of the number of bridesmaids and ushers who are chosen.

You may select a married friend or relative to participate without feeling obligated to have the groom ask the husband of your selection to be part of his wedding party. If you select younger participants, between the ages of eight and sixteen years old, they become junior bridesmaids and they are given as much responsibility as you feel they can adequately handle. They do not give showers or stand in the receiving line unless you specifically ask them to. Whether they attend showers and parties and participate at the rehearsal dinner is up to you. They walk first in the processional and do not require a partner in the recessional (unless the groom has selected junior groomsmen as well).

At one time, it was totally unacceptable to consider having a pregnant friend or relative participate in the wedding party but pregnancy no longer automatically rules out someone special. All you need do when asking a pregnant friend is simply remember to take into consideration all of the possibilities, such as how close the actual wedding date is to the delivery date, how can the bridesmaids' dresses be modified to a maternity dress, or what type of dress will coordinate nicely. Make certain that you speak openly with the pregnant party and confirm that she will not feel self-conscious.

The greatest gift of life is friendship and I have received it.

Hubert Humphrey

Responsibilities

1. The bridesmaids assist you and the maid/ matron-of-honor with any pre-wedding tasks that need to be completed.

2. They usually pay for their own wedding attire and all accessories, except flowers, as well as their own travel expenses (except for hotel accommodations which should be paid by you unless other arrangements are made in advance).

3. They often give you a shower or party and they attend all pre-wedding parties that they are invited to. The obligation of gifts is the same as it is for the maid/matron-of-honor; see page 16. Some-times they will give you a joint gift that has all of their initials engraved as a thank you and memento.

4. They attend the rehearsal and rehearsal dinner.

5. Unless you are having the flowers delivered to the wedding site, they are responsible for picking up their bouquets at your home or a prearranged location two hours before the ceremony.

6. They take part in the wedding procession, the recession, and usually stand at the maid/ matron-of-honor's side during the ceremony.

7. If you elect to have them stand in the receiving line, they stand next to you if the maid/matron-of-honor is on the groom's left or next to the maid-of-honor if she is standing next to you.

8. They sit alternately with the ushers at the bride's table if there is to be a formal sit-down dinner.

9. All bridesmaids must stay available for formal pictures before and after the ceremony and during the reception.

10. They mingle with the guests and take part in all of the reception activities. If there is a traditional first dance, the bridesmaids dance with the ushers at the appropriate time. During the bouquet-throwing ceremony, if they are single, they participate, but all bridesmaids should take it upon themselves to encourage other single guests to participate as well.

11. You may ask each of them individually to help the maid/matron-of-honor with arrangements after you depart from the reception and until you return from your honeymoon. For example, one bridesmaid may make certain your wedding gown is properly cared for until your return, one may make certain all of the gifts are delivered to a prearranged location, and one may care for your bouquet or take it to a florist for preserving.

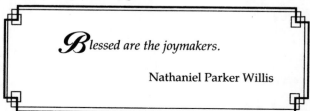

ℬlessed are the joymakers.

Nathaniel Parker Willis

Bride's Checklist for Bridesmaids

Bridesmaid_____

Phone_____

Address_____

Travel Arrangements_____

Accommodations_____

Special Duties_____

Bridesmaid_____

Phone_____

Address_____

Travel Arrangements_____

Accommodations_____

Special Duties_____

Bridesmaid_____

Phone_____

Address_____

Travel Arrangements_____

Accommodations_____

Special Duties_____

Bridesmaid_____

Phone_____

Address_____

Travel Arrangements_____

Accommodations_____

Special Duties_____

Notes

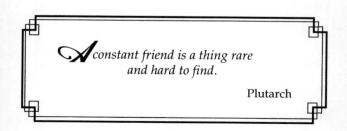

*A constant friend is a thing rare
and hard to find.*

Plutarch

Groomsmen

Traditionally, a groomsman was selected by the groom as an escort for a bridesmaid and an usher was at the wedding strictly to seat guests before the ceremony. And the rule of thumb was to have one usher for every fifty guests, assuming that one-half to three-fourths of your invited guests will attend. In today's society, however, the roles are combined, the terms are used interchangeably and there may be any number you and the groom desire.

The groom may choose to have one groomsman for each of your bridesmaids and then ask additional individuals to be ushers, naming one the head usher. Another option is to have all groomsmen serve as ushers, seating guests before the ceremony, and joining the wedding party shortly before the ceremony. Still another choice is to have groomsmen usher, then join the wedding party, and to have a head usher who remains behind to seat late arrivals, assist the best man with his duties, and to supervise special arrangements. Junior ushers (ages eight to sixteen) may be assigned the same duties as older ushers, perhaps walking in the processional and recessional, or simply standing near the entrance to the ceremony site to seat late arrivals.

It is a nice gesture for the groom to ask a member of your family to be one of his groomsmen or an usher. These men are usually the groom's brothers, relatives, friends, and your brothers.

Responsibilities ————————————————

1. One particularly reliable usher is appointed the head usher by the groom. He helps the best man supervise the other ushers and is responsible for any tasks the best man assigns to him. He assigns the other ushers certain aisles, he is in charge of special seating arrangements, and has a pew seating chart available in case of questions or forgotten pew cards. It is the head usher who identifies special guests, such as a favorite aunt or old family friends, and sees they are seated toward the front.

2. All of the groomsmen are usually responsible to pick up, pay for, or rent their own wedding attire and all accessories (except their gloves, neckwear and boutonnieres which are given to them by the groom). They pay for their own travel expenses (except for hotel accommodations which should be paid by the groom unless other arrangements are made).

3. They attend all pre-wedding parties to which they are invited and the rehearsal and rehearsal dinner, and may, singly or jointly with the best man, host the bachelors' party or other pre-wedding parties.

4. All groomsmen contribute to a joint gift to the groom which is traditionally selected and presented by the best man.

5. They should arrive at the wedding site approximately one hour before the ceremony begins.

6. Groomsmen seat arriving guests before the ceremony, asking if they are friends or relatives of the bride or groom and making polite but quiet conversation with the guests as they are escorted to their seats. They offer their right arm to each woman while her escort follows behind. If several women arrive together, the eldest should be seated first. An elderly man alone may also be accompanied to his seat by an usher. Traditionally, the bride's guests are on the left, the groom's on the right (the opposite is true in a Jewish service). If one section has many more guests than the other, the usher will seat the guests on the side with more available seats. (For more detailed information on ceremony seating, see *Wedding Ceremonies* by Jo Packham, page 75).

7. If one of the ushers is a brother of yours or the groom, he will be the one to escort his own mother to her proper place. If not, the head usher will seat your mother in the left front pew and the groom's parents in the right front pew. The groom's parents are to be seated five minutes before your mother. When your mother is seated, it is a signal that the processional is about to begin and no other guests are to be seated after that time.

If either your parents or the groom's parents are divorced, the mother and her husband sit in the first pew and the father and his wife sit in the second pew (unless you feel it is appropriate to have both parents and spouses sit together.)

8. One or several of the groomsmen may perform other pre-ceremony functions such as distributing programs, rolling out an aisle runner, or setting up pew ribbons.

9. Groomsmen precede or escort, whichever style you prefer, the bridesmaids down the aisle during the processional and escort the bridesmaids during the recessional.

10. One or several of the ushers should return to the front of the church after the recessional to loosen the pew ribbons; escort your mother and the groom's mother, honored elderly, or disabled guests out of the church first; and then return and signal the other guests to file out, row by row, from front to back.

11. An appointed usher makes certain that all belongings of the wedding party and guests have been cleared before leaving the ceremony site.

12. Ushers give directions to the reception site and make certain that all guests have transportation.

13. The ushers transport bridesmaids and out-of-town guests throughout the wedding day, if it is necessary.

14. Ushers sit at the bridal table alternating with the bridesmaids.

15. Unless instructed otherwise by you, the groomsmen do not stand in the receiving line but mingle with the guests, dancing with the bridesmaids and any single female guests who may be in attendance. Ushers also are to participate in all reception activities and should encourage single men to participate in the garter ceremony.

16. It is the ushers' responsibility to help in any capacity whenever needed during both the ceremony and the reception.

17. All stay available for formal pictures before or after the ceremony and during the reception.

18. They help other wedding party members with post-reception duties such as making sure all gifts are transferred to a secure location, making certain that all of the flowers are delivered, and help to check that nothing is left behind at the reception site.

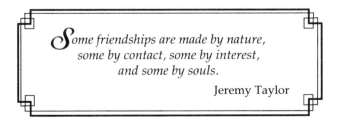

*Some friendships are made by nature,
some by contact, some by interest,
and some by souls.*

Jeremy Taylor

Checklist for Groomsmen

Groomsman_____

Phone_____

Address_____

Travel Arrangements_____

Accommodations_____

Special Duties_____

Groomsman_____

Phone_____

Address_____

Travel Arrangements_____

Accommodations_____

Special Duties_____

Groomsman_____

Phone_____

Address_____

Travel Arrangements_____

Accommodations_____

Special Duties_____

Groomsman_____

Phone_____

Address_____

Travel Arrangements_____

Accommodations_____

Special Duties_____

Head Usher_____

Phone_____

Address_____

Travel Arrangements_____

Accommodations_____

Special Duties_____

Reserved Section Seat Chart
for Head Usher

FIRST PEW
Bride's Section_____

_____

_____

_____

Groom's Section_____

_____

_____

_____

SECOND PEW

Bride's Section_____

_____

_____

_____

Groom's Section_____

_____

_____

_____

THIRD PEW

Bride's Section_____

_____

_____

_____

Groom's Section_____

_____

_____

_____

Child Attendants

Children can add a great deal of charm to wedding festivities and, if this is a second marriage, it may be essential that they are included in all phases of the activities. Due to their unpredictably, you may elect to include no more than two child attendants. It is, however, a decision that you and the groom should make, depending on how many young children you want to have involved and how much help you can solicit to keep them supervised and entertained.

Child attendants are usually between four and eight years of age. If you elect to have attendants between these ages, or children even younger than four years old, participate, you will need to make some alternate plans. If you feel they are too young to stand quietly during the ceremony, direct them to slip into the pew with their parents and be seated during the ceremony. If they are seated during the ceremony, they do not participate in the recessional. Do not give any child attendant a task where there could be problems if the task remains uncompleted, and make certain that their parents are invited to all activities and understand that they are to closely supervise their offspring.

The child attendants should be invited to the rehearsal but probably not the rehearsal dinner. They should, however, be included in all of the activities during the reception—children will especially love being the center of attention and showing off their new clothing. If there is to be a sit-down dinner at the reception, the child attendants sit with their parents unless there is a special children's table with an adult supervisor nearby. Always remember that they will need to be closely supervised during the entire reception. To allow their parents and other members of the wedding party to enjoy themselves at the reception, you may elect to hire someone specifically to watch smaller children. Give each child a gift that he or she can play with and designate a specific area for them to play in. Do not give the person supervising the children an impossible job of supervising children at an adult gathering without something and somewhere to keep them entertained.

Flower Girl

Nothing is more delightful than a young girl dressed in wedding finery! If the flower girl carries a bouquet, make sure it is as pretty on the back as it is on the front because a child's style for carrying the bouquet is quite unpredictable. In place of a bouquet, she may carry a small basket filled with flowers or rose petals to strew on the bride's path ahead. (Some reception sites currently refuse to allow this practice because of liability so be certain to check beforehand.)

She may walk alone, with the ring bearer, or with another flower girl of about the same height, but she always comes immediately before you and your father in the procession.

During the ceremony, she stands between the maid/matron-of-honor and the first attendant. If the flower girl is too young to stand quietly throughout the ceremony, an easy-to-follow plan should be worked out. For example, she may join her parents in their pew, as long as she can find them very easily. Another choice would be for her to slip into the far end of the first pew. Depending upon the site, a small chair could be inconspicuously placed near the front for her. At any rate, be sure everyone knows the plan, especially the flower girl.

In the recessional, she is escorted by the ring bearer and they both follow immediately behind you and the groom.

Her parents are responsible for her attire and accessories, except the flowers.

She may be included with the bridesmaids in rehearsal, transportation, and photography arrangements, or her parents may be asked to be responsible for making certain she has adequate transportation to a scheduled photography session, to the rehearsal, the ceremony, and the reception.

Ring Bearer

The ring bearer is traditionally a boy (but, as a contemporary bride, you may choose a girl) who carries a satin pillow with two rings, yours and the groom's, tied or sewn onto it. The satin pillow should be made exactly the same on both sides with the rings being attached to only one side. These may be symbolic rings, with the honor attendants holding the actual rings. After the ceremony, the cushion is turned upside down so the symbolic rings do not show. If you choose to use your wedding rings, they should be tied securely to the pillow top. The ring bearer simply holds the pillow while the maid/matron-of-honor or the best man unties the appropriate ring.

The ring bearer may walk down the aisle beside the flower girl or he may walk alone, in which case he precedes her. He stands between the best man and the first groomsman during the ceremony. In the recessional, he escorts the flower girl, following behind you and the groom. Just as with the flower girl, if the ring bearer is too young to stand through the ceremony, make specific arrangements for an alternative plan.

His parents are, also, responsible for his attire and accessories (except the cushion). Ring bearers, as well as other male participants, might wear a scaled down version of the men's formal wear or you may select something totally different but complementary.

Pages or Train Bearers

Pages or train bearers may be appointed at a very formal wedding to carry your cathedral-length train down the aisle. Traditionally two boys of the same height are chosen, but as a contemporary bride you may elect to choose two girls, or a boy and a girl. Plan a place for them to stand during the ceremony, depending upon the site. They may be needed to assist you with your train before the recessional and should be instructed to either slip into a pew or follow you down the aisle. Their parents are responsible for their attire and accessories.

Candlelighters

Candlelighters are often two boys from either family who light the candles just before the mother of the bride is seated. Here again, however, you may choose two girls or a boy and a girl. They are then seated with their parents in places of honor before the ceremony begins. Their parents are responsible for their attire and accessories.

Give all to love ...

Emerson

Checklist for Child Attendants

Flower Girl_____

Parents_____

Address_____

Phone_____

Transportation_____

Special Duties_____

Ring Bearer_____

Parents_____

Address_____

Phone_____

Transportation_____

Special Duties_____

Pages or Train Bearers_____

Parents_____

Address_____

Phone_____

Transportation_____

Special Duties_____

Candlelighters_____

_____

_____

_____

Parents_____

Address_____

Phone_____

Transportation_____

Special Duties _____

Notes

Letter to Attendants

Below is a letter you may wish to use to communicate what you are expecting from each wedding participant. You may put this letter into a computer and then personalize all the information for each person. Regardless, a handwritten note will be a nice addition to this correspondence.

Dear_____,

Thank you for all of your help and support. Enclosed you will find a copy of agendas to help you. I have listed all of the details and your responsibilities below.

If you have any questions, please call me. Thank you again for all that you are doing.

Fitting Dates
First Fitting Date _____

Final Fitting Date_____

Location(s) _____

Time _____

Phone _____

Notes _____

Rehearsal at Ceremony Site

Date _____

Time _____

Address _____

Rehearsal Dinner Party

Date _____

Time _____

Location _____

Attire _____

Ceremony

Arrival Time _____

Where to Dress _____

Transportation _____

Photo Session

Location _____

Time _____

Photos to Be Included in _____

_____

_____

Reception
Location _____

Time _____

Transportation_____

Receiving Line_____

Individual Responsibilities
Before the Ceremony _____

_____

_____

_____

During the Ceremony_____

_____

_____

_____

During the Reception_____

_____

_____

_____

After the Reception _____

_____

_____

_____

Important Phone Numbers

Bride _____

Bride's Parents _____

Groom _____

Groom's Parents _____

Other _____

_____

Notes

Joy, gentle friends!
Joy & fresh days of love accompany
your hearts!

Shakespeare

Persons of Honor or Special Helpers

Special people, who are not members of your wedding party, need not be left out. There are a myriad of ways to involve them during the ceremony or the reception. Consider assigning close friends, family members, or relatives tasks such as:

- Offering them a special toast during the reception.

- Reading a selected scripture, poem, or excerpt during the ceremony or participating in sentence prayers (each adding a line to continue the prayer).

- Singing during the ceremony.

- Asking for their help with decorations.

- Handing out ceremony programs, mass books, or yarmulkes.

- Greeting guests at the reception by sitting at the guest book.

- Taking charge of the gift table.

- Serving refreshments during the reception or passing out the groom's cake.

- Passing out packets of rice for your departure ceremony.

Checklist for Persons of Honor

Position_____

Name_____

Address_____

Phone_____

Arrival Time _____

Special Duty_____

Position_____

Name_____

Address_____

Phone_____

Arrival Time _____

Special Duty_____

Position_____

Name_____

Address_____

Phone_____

Arrival Time _____

Special Duty_____

> $y$ou do not choose your family.
> They are God's gift to you,
> as you are to them.
>
> Desmond Tutu

Family Members

Your wedding is a memorable and momentous occasion for your parents as well as for you. It is a time when you can become even closer to them by involving them in as many aspects of the wedding plans as you feel comfortable.

Remember that their feelings are as varied as yours—the range goes from the exhilaration of seeing you so happy and full of hope for the future to the sadness of "losing" you to someone else. Be careful of their feelings, be considerate of their suggestions, and be confident of the fact that their offer of involvement is meant to help you and make you happy.

Your Mother

Depending upon your age, the physical and emotional closeness between you and your mother, and your own feelings of how much involvement you want or need from family members, your mother may be asked to help with any or all of the tasks listed below.

If you will be traveling to your parents' hometown just for the wedding and the reception, you will probably count on your mother to do most of the on-site planning. It will help if you purchase two identical wedding journals and keep in constant communication— there will be more questions and details than you ever dreamed of!

1. Your mother compiles the guest list for your side of the family and helps address the invitations.

2. She arranges as many details of the ceremony and the reception as you wish her to. This can go from total control of the arrangements to merely offering her opinion.

3. She helps you select whatever it is that you want help selecting—for example, your wedding outfit, trousseau, invitations, wedding flowers, or bridal registry items.

4. She undertakes any important errands that you need help with.

5. If the groom and his family are from out of town, your mother makes their hotel reservations as well as any reservations for out-of-town groomsmen. (The groom's family is, however, responsible for all bills.) She also makes any necessary reservations for out-of-town relatives and friends (who are responsible for their own travel and accommodation expenses).

6. She attends all pre-wedding showers and parties that she is invited to as well as the rehearsal and rehearsal dinner.

7. Your mother provides friends with information about gift registry and any personal preferences you and the groom have.

8. She helps keep track of your gifts and arranges to have them displayed in a safe place, if you wish her to do so.

9. She keeps your father and the groom's parents posted as to the progress of the wedding plans. If the groom's parents are from out of town, she keeps them posted on all events, sends them any newspaper articles, and may try to help them feel involved by sending a note listing which gifts have arrived or an account of the parties that have been given.

10. Your mother informs the groom's mother of her wedding attire selection so the groom's mother will select a dress or gown similar in style and color.

11. She may assist you in dressing the day of the ceremony.

12. Your mother is the official hostess for your wedding, unless you are older or this is your second marriage. In either of these cases, you may still select her to be the hostess to honor her. As official hostess, she attends to any emergency that might occur during the ceremony or reception. She may enlist the aid of your father, the maid/matron-of-honor, or the best man.

13. She is privileged to be seated last before the ceremony is to begin and in the front pew on your side of the aisle. She will stand just before you and your father walk down the aisle, signaling to other guests that they should also rise. She is the first to be ushered out following the recessional.

14. If she is the hostess during the reception, she greets all of the guests at the head of the receiving line (or at the front door if it is to be a small home wedding). She also is responsible for many of the introductions between guests.

15. She sits in a place of honor at the parents' table during the reception dinner.

16. She stations herself so that she can thank the guests and say good-bye as everyone leaves.

Mother's Checklist

Special Duties_____

_____

_____

_____

_____

_____

_____

_____

_____

_____

_____

_____

_____

_____

_____

_____

_____

_____

_____

Your Father ────────────

Your father will act as the official host with your mother unless you elect otherwise. He may be the one wedding participant who feels most "forgotten" during the majority of pre-wedding festivities so you will want to make a concentrated effort to include him and share with him all of the wonderful events that are taking place in your honor.

It is especially nice for the two of you if you set aside an afternoon every three or four weeks to have a quiet lunch together to share all your hopes, emotions, and joys.

1. He attends all pre-wedding parties that he is invited to, including the rehearsal and rehearsal dinner.

2. If your parents are divorced, your father is responsible for his own guest list.

3. If there is no wedding coordinator, he and your mother go over all of the arrangements a day or two before the wedding so that he can attend to any emergencies should they arise. If he is not clear as to what happens when, he may not know that, for example, the flowers were to be delivered at two o'clock and the fact that they are not there constitutes an emergency.

4. He rides with you to the ceremony, if you are having a formal wedding, or if you decide that you just want him to do so, regardless of the size of the guest list.

5. He escorts you down the aisle and sits in the first pew next to your mother. If your mother and father are divorced and friendly, whether he is remarried or not, he sits next to your mother. If they are not friendly, and one or both have remarried, your mother sits in the first pew and your father sits in the second pew.

6. He may or may not stand in the receiving line next to your mother. If he does not, he mingles with the guests and checks to make certain all is proceeding with the arrangements.

7. He is in charge of the bar and champagne supply. Along with your mother and the best man, he attends to any emergencies that might occur during the ceremony or the reception.

8. He dances with you immediately after the groom.

9. He usually makes a short toast or welcoming speech after the best man, if there is a formal sit-down dinner.

10. He stands with your mother at the end of the reception to say good-bye to all of the guests and thank them for coming and he is always the last person to leave.

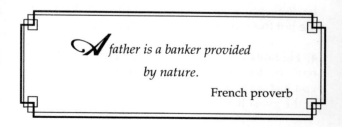

A father is a banker provided

by nature.

French proverb

Father's Checklist

Special Duties_____

_____

_____

_____

_____

_____

_____

_____

_____

_____

_____

_____

_____

_____

_____

_____

_____

_____

_____

_____

_____

The Groom's Parents ─────────

Even though, traditionally, the role played by the groom's parents is smaller than that of your parents, they should still be treated with equal respect and an additional effort should be made to involve them and keep them abreast of all the activities from the first announcement to the final good-bye at the end of the reception. The groom's parents' responsibilities are as follows:

1. They contact your parents first after the announcement to welcome you and your parents into their family.

2. The groom's parents may wish to send you an engagement gift. It is usually something very sentimental such as a piece of family jewelry.

3. The groom's mother produces the wedding list for the groom's side of the family and gives it to your mother as soon as possible. She should include a separate list with all out-of-town guests and invited relatives so that your mother can make the necessary seating arrangements for the ceremony and the reception dinner. Usually they contribute equally to the guest list and may or may not offer to share expenses. If they wish to invite a substantially larger number of guests than your parents, you need to discuss an equable way to divide expenses. (For more information on this subject, see page 66.)

4. The groom's mother should be invited to all of the pre-wedding parties and showers that your mother is invited to, even if she lives too far away to attend.

5. The groom's parents usually host and pay for the rehearsal dinner. They are, of course, included in the rehearsal also.

6. They consult with your parents on the proper wedding attire so that both their attire is complementary.

7. They make accommodations for the groom's out-of-town wedding participants and out-of-town guests (who are responsible for their own hotel accommodations unless other arrangements are made.)

8. If they are from out of town, they give all of the necessary information about their stay to your mother so she can make accommodations and reservations (even though they are responsible to pay for them.)

9. They are honored guests at the ceremony and are seated in the first pew on the groom's side of the church about five minutes before your mother.

10. The groom's mother always stands in the receiving line but the groom's father's participation is optional. He may choose to mingle with the guests. If both do opt to stand in the receiving line, the groom's mother stands next to your mother and the father stands next to you. The groom's parents are responsible for introducing their guests to your family and other guests.

11. The groom's father dances with you following your dance with the groom and your father.

12. If they do not participate financially in the wedding, they should always send a very formal thank you to your parents immediately following the festivities. If they do participate financially, a thank you is still appropriate for your family's contribution to a very successful event.

13. If the groom's parents share equally in the wedding expenses, then their roles and responsibilities become the same as your parents.

*K*ind hearts are the garden.
Kind thoughts are the roots.
Kind words are the blossoms.
Kind deeds are the fruit.

John Ruskin

Divorced Parents & Stepparents

When parents are divorced and may be remarried, a myriad of emotions can come to the surface. You need to be conscious of the feelings of both sets of parents and stepparents, communicate with everyone honestly and openly, and do what you believe is necessary to not only make you happy but to make the entire affair comfortable and memorable for them as well.

If everyone is friendly, the decisions are easy ones; if everyone is not friendly, take one situation at a time and make the decisions and arrangements that will keep both sets of parents and stepparents separated as much as possible, all the while making both feel equally important and loved.

If one of the stepparents is particularly close to you or the groom and if one stepparent finances or contributes to the wedding festivities, then he or she, with your parents, will be acting hosts for the wedding. The stepparent, nevertheless, should still allow the natural parents to be the focal hosts of the event unless there are some extenuating circumstances.

Traditional Expenses

One of the most delicate and yet most important questions in all of your wedding planning will be "Who pays for what?"

Regardless of how the wedding festivities are to be financed, you and your fiancé need to sit down and talk frankly, deciding how you want your wedding to be. If you need help from parents, listen to their suggestions but do not let them dictate the style of the wedding or change your plans. It is still your wedding and it should be exactly as you want it to be.

These lists can be modified to suit your personal wants and needs. Any combination of sharing expenses between you, the groom, your parents, his parents, and the wedding party can be implemented with everyone's consent. Just be sure to discuss all costs early and openly so each party knows what you are expecting of them.

Expenses for You & Your Parents

1. The announcement party, if they host it.

2. The invitations, announcements, enclosure cards, and personal stationery, including stamps for mailing.

3. Your wedding dress, veil, and accessories.

4. Your trousseau of clothes and lingerie.

5. Their own wedding attire and the attire required for any family members still living at home.

6. The groom's ring.

7. Any bridal consultant fees.

8. Hotel accommodations for any of your attendants.

9. All expenses of the ceremony, except for those listed otherwise; see page 70.
   a. Rental fee for the church or ceremony site.
   b. Fees for any additional equipment such as aisle carpets, candle holders, etc.

10. Fees for all ceremony participants (other than family members, friends, or relatives) such as the organist, soloist, or band members. This does not include the ceremony official.

11. All expenses of the reception.
   a. Rental fee for the reception site.
   b. All food and beverage charges.
   c. All catering charges.
   d. The wedding cake or cakes.
   e. Music for the reception.
   f. Fees for such items as guest book, wedding gift book, etc.

12. The following flowers:
   a. All flowers used for decorating the ceremony and reception sites.
   b. Bouquets or corsages for the bridesmaids, honor attendants, and the flower girl.

c. Flowers or corsages for any other wedding participants in addition to the wedding party.

d. Corsages or flowers given to any special relatives or friends who may have helped.

e. Flowers sent to any hostess who entertained for you or for you and the groom before your wedding day.

13. A wedding gift for you and the groom.

14. Gifts for your attendants.

15. Your photograph taken before the ceremony.

16. All photography, and any recordings or videotaping of the ceremony or reception.

17. All charges for transporting the bridal party to the church and from the church to the reception site.

18. All expenses involved in parking cars, security, and traffic control.

19. Any extra help employed to assist with the wedding or the reception.

Expenses for the Groom
& the Groom's Parents

1. Your engagement and wedding rings.

2. Marriage license.

3. Their personal wedding attire and accessories.

4. Gloves, ties, and ascots for all men in the wedding party.

5. Hotel accommodations for the groom's out-of-town groomsmen.

6. The rehearsal dinner.

7. Ceremony official's fee.

8. A wedding gift for you and the groom.

9. Your flowers, including going-away corsages and throwing bouquet.

10. Groom's boutonniere and those for his groomsmen.

11. Corsages for mothers and grandmothers.

12. Gifts for the best man and attendants.

13. Complete honeymoon trip.

> *T*he gown is hers that
> wears it, and the world
> is his that enjoys it.
>
> Proverb

Attire for the Wedding Party

The size of the wedding, the time of day, and the location will determine the formality and style of your gown as well as what everyone else involved in the wedding party will wear.

The following chart offers basic outlines for four basic types of wedding styles. Styles may be combined or adjusted to suit your needs and wants and can be somewhat different in different regions due to local customs, religious mandates, or ethnic heritages.

	Very Formal	Formal	Semiformal	Informal
Style	Traditional, expensive, elaborate	More relaxed, most popular	Between formal and informal	Whatever you desire
Invitations/Announcements	Engraved on heavy, white or ivory paper; card folded; two envelopes; enclosures.	Engraved or printed on heavy, white or ivory paper; single or folded card– one or two envelopes; enclosures.	Printed on any color paper, additions such as photographs; one envelope	Printed, hand-written on any color paper or style that is appropriate is acceptable.
Ceremony	Church, synagogue, temple, ballroom	Church, synagogue, temple, ballroom, home, country club	Anywhere that is appropriate	Anywhere desired
Reception	Large, lavish dinner and music	Dinner and music	Usually includes meal, maybe music	Small and simple
Food/Beverages	Champagne, wine or liquor and assorted beverages Sit-down or large buffet, bridal party and guests have tables	Champagne or punch, other drinks optional Buffet, bridal party may have tables	Champagne for toasts, other drinks optional Stand-up buffet	Champagne for toasts, tea, coffee, other drinks optional Snacks or cake

	Very Formal	Formal	Semiformal	Informal
Decorations/Accessories	Elaborate flowers for church and reception. Canopy, pew ribbons, aisle carpet, limousines, groom's cake, engraved napkins	Flowers for church and reception Limousines and other items optional	Flowers for altar, some decorations for reception	Whatever you desire
Music	Organ at church, soloist optional, dancing at reception	Organ at church, soloist optional, dancing optional	Organ at church	Usually no music
Guest List	Over 200 guests	75–200 guests	Under 100 guests	Not more than 50 guests
Bride	Elegant, long dress, long sleeves/ gloves, long train, veil	Long dress, any sleeve length, veil, shorter train	Morning wedding-knee length Evening-floor length, veil/hat/ wreath	Dress or suit or whatever you desire
Females	6–8 attendants, long dress	2–6 attendants, long dress	1–3 attendants, dress based on length, style of bride's	1 attendant, dress or suit or casual
Males	Cutaway, long jacket or stroller for day; tailcoat for night	Cutaway, stroller or tuxedo for day; tuxedo for night	Stroller, tuxedo, dinner jacket for day; tuxedo, dinner jacket, suit or blazer for evening	Business suit, blazer

Bridesmaids' Attire

Naturally, you will want your attendants dressed in attire that matches the style of your wedding but you will also want to select gowns that they will feel comfortable wearing and that they can perhaps wear on other occasions. It is especially important to take this into consideration because they will be paying for their own gowns and accessories. You may even want to gather all of your attendants together and ask their opinions so you are certain everyone is as happy with the selections as you are. If it is possible, it is often a very nice gesture to invite everyone to lunch and discuss style, color, and accessories. Then you can go shopping by yourself and select three or four styles you think they will like. Gather everyone together a second time, escort them to the places where you found the gowns, and then let them vote on which they prefer.

If any of your attendants are from out of town, you may have to send them drawings or pictures of the gowns you have selected, or color swatches for them to use in selecting their own gowns. If you have selected a specific dress, you can order one for them in their size and then send it to them so they can have it altered. You can also ask your salesperson for the style number, color number, name and phone number of the manufacturer and your attendants can take this information to a bridal shop in their town, be measured there, and they can order the gown themselves.

Traditionally, the maid/matron-of-honor had one style or color of dress with all of the bridesmaids having a slightly different style in the same color or the same dress in a different color. The flower girl had a coordinating dress. It is becoming more and more common, however, for you to select a color for the wedding and have the maid/matron-of-honor and the bridesmaids choose a dress in the style each is most comfortable wearing, using the color you have selected. You are then guaranteed that each will like her dress, will be able to wear it again after the wedding, and that paying for it will probably never be an issue. If you have definite ideas on what their dresses should be and they are a somewhat unusual color or style, you should probably pay for the dresses and the accessories yourself; then it will not matter as much if they are never worn again.

The junior bridesmaids' dresses may be identical to, or blend with, the attendants' gowns. You may choose to take the same basic pattern and alter it with ruffles, or ribbons. Flats or ballet slippers are most appropriate.

The attendants' accessories are as important as their gowns. Will they be wearing headpieces such as flower bands or hats? Should all of their shoes be identical or just the same color? Do they need gloves or special undergarments? Are they allowed to wear jewelry? If your wedding is to be a formal one, you may choose to give one of the accessories as a gift to your attendants. An engraved locket or a special bracelet might be the final, perfect touch.

Flower Girl

The flower girl wears a long or short dress that matches or complements the style and color of the others.

Mothers

Mothers usually wear full-length dresses except for the most informal daytime weddings. Your mother makes her choice first, then discusses colors and styles with the groom's mother. Their dresses should be complementary with all other wedding party members.

Special Helpers

Special helpers or honored persons should wear attire that is also complementary in color and style to the wedding party. They will want to dress subtly so as not to upstage the bride and her attendants.

Traditional guidelines are used as a basis for the selection of your wedding attendants' gowns and accessories. As with every other guideline listed in this book, there is no reason you cannot change, combine, or delete any option to fit your own needs.

Female Wedding Party Attire Checklist

Maid/Matron-of-Honor_____

Description of Dress_____

Size_____

Where Purchased_____

Salesperson_____

Cost_____

Fitting Date/Time_____

Headpiece_____

Shoes_____

Accessories_____

Delivery Date_____

Deposit_____

Balance Due_____

Bridesmaid_____

Description of Dress_____

Size_____

Where Purchased_____

Salesperson_____

Cost _____

Fitting Date/Time_____

Headpiece_____

Shoes_____

Accessories_____

Delivery Date_____

Deposit _____

Balance Due _____

Bridesmaid_____

Description of Dress_____

Size_____

Where Purchased_____

Salesperson_____

Cost _____

Fitting Date/Time_____

Headpiece_____

Shoes_____

Accessories_____

Delivery Date_____

Deposit _____

Balance Due _____

Bridesmaid_____

Description of Dress_____

Size_____

Where Purchased_____

Salesperson_____

Cost _____

Fitting Date/Time_____

Headpiece_____

Shoes_____

Accessories_____

Delivery Date_____

Deposit _____

Balance Due _____

Flower Girl_____

Size_____

Where Purchased_____

Salesperson_____

Cost_____

Fitting Date/Time_____

Headpiece_____

Shoes_____

Accessories_____

Delivery Date_____

Deposit_____

Balance Due_____

Men's Attire

The type of clothing and the accessories that the groom and other male members of the wedding party will wear depends again upon the style you have selected for the wedding.

For a formal wedding, it is the most common practice for all of the men in the wedding party, including both fathers, to rent formal clothing for the day. These suits should all be obtained from the same shop to avoid any confusion or mistakes.

It is often a good idea for you and the groom to initially shop for the male attire together. If either of you has very definite ideas, it will be much easier to compromise if you have several choices in front of you rather than disagreeing on concepts. When selecting a shop from which to rent, you need to find one that is dependable. You can ask friends, a wedding consultant, or check the yellow pages for possible locations. Check the professionalism of the shop by inspecting it in person. Is it clean and well maintained? Is the clothing a reasonable price? Do they carry nationally known labels and designers? Is the personnel friendly and well informed? It is very important that the salesperson understands how to accurately take measurements, that you inspect the clothing on hand and see that it is not worn, and that you receive a guarantee that the outfits will be properly altered, cleaned and pressed. Never, never take for granted that the outfits will fit perfectly; they must be fitted individually. If one or more of the male attendants is from out of town, have them go to their local formal-wear shop to be measured and send the measurements to you for the initial order. They will need to arrive two days early so that they can accompany you and in-town attendants to be fitted one final time before the ceremony. This allows adequate time to have last-minute alterations made. It does not matter how expensive the tuxedo, if it does not fit properly it can be a source of embarrassment and discomfort for both you and the grooms-man.

For best results, do the initial shopping about six months before the wedding, especially if the wedding is during the spring or the peak summer months or during a holiday. Try to have the groom visit more than one store so that he is certain he is ordering exactly what he wants at the best price. If you do not accompany the groom to select the style of attire, make certain he has a written, detailed description of your gown, including style and color, as well as a description of your attendants' gowns. The men's wear is supposed to complement the womens' apparel. The groom should also be given swatches of material to use to match colors. For example, if your gown is ivory, his formal wear should never be stark white.

The final look of his ensemble and that of his attendants is determined by the cut of the coat and its lapels, type of shirt, neckwear, and vest or cummerbund as well as the fabric of the clothing and the colors in the outfit; the chart on page 73 offers some guidelines.

Men's Attire Checklist

Men's formal-wear store _____

Fitting Date/Time _____

Date Ready _____

Date to Be Returned _____

Groom   Size

Trousers _____

Shirt _____

Coat _____

Vest/Cummerbund _____

Neckwear _____

Collar _____

Other (suspenders, cuff links, studs, pocket squares)

_____

_____

Shoes _____

Rental Fee _____

Size

Best Man_____

Trousers_____

Shirt_____

Coat_____

Vest/Cummerbund_____

Neckwear _____

Collar_____

Other (suspenders, cuff links, studs, pocket squares)

_____

_____

Shoes _____

Rental Fee _____

Size

Groomsman_____

Trousers_____

Shirt_____

Coat_____

Vest/Cummerbund_____

Neckwear _____

Collar_____

Other (suspenders, cuff links, studs, pocket squares)

_____

_____

Shoes _____

Rental Fee _____

                                                    Size

Groomsman_____

Trousers_____

Shirt_____

Coat_____

Vest/Cummerbund_____

Neckwear _____

Collar_____

Other (suspenders, cuff links, studs, pocket squares)

_____

_____

Shoes _____

Rental Fee _____

Size

Groomsman_____

Trousers_____

Shirt_____

Coat_____

Vest/Cummerbund_____

Neckwear _____

Collar_____

Other (suspenders, cuff links, studs, pocket squares)

_____

_____

Shoes _____

Rental Fee _____

> *Gratitude takes three forms: a feeling in the heart, an expression in words, and a giving in return.*
>
> Unknown

Gifts for the Wedding Party

The gifts you give to all of those who participated in your wedding are a small, yet sincere, way of saying thank you to everyone who helped make your most memorable day all that you had dreamed it would be.

Your gifts need not be expensive. They need only to be thoughtful and lasting. A little creativity and advance planning can insure that your gifts really say what you want them to say.

Traditionally, you present your gift to your attendants at the bridesmaids' party. If you have opted not to have such a party, you may present your gifts at the rehearsal dinner or any other special occasion before the ceremony. Gifts to your attendants are usually the same item or the same in quality and price, with the honor attendants' gift being slightly different. They should be permanent items of a personal nature that somehow relate to this special day. Some ideas are a silver picture frame with the promise of a picture of all of the attendants together to be given after the wedding, an engraved silver pen, or a pair of engraved silver wine goblets. If the wedding is to be a formal one, you may choose to give your attendants an accessory item that would complement their dresses. An engraved locket or a lovely bracelet would be something they could wear and treasure always.

Gifts that the groom presents to his attendants are traditionally given during the bachelors' party. If, however, the evening's activities are planned to be on the wild side, they might be lost or broken and certainly not fully appreciated. Under these circumstances, the groom will want to synchronize his gift-giving with you and choose the rehearsal dinner as a better time. Such gifts should be similar to your attendants' gifts and should be personal and lasting in nature. They could include engraved money clips, hand-tooled leather wallets, monogrammed bathrobes, or fashionable pens. If the wedding is formal, the groom will also give his attendants the ties, gloves, and ascots that they will wear.

A small gift should be given to the flower girl and the ring bearer. You are responsible for the flower girl's gift, and the groom buys the ring bearer's gift.

If you are giving engraved items, it is sometimes suggested that you give something with the wedding date or your and the groom's initials on it. This author believes, however, that it is much more sentimental and something that can be worn more easily if the engraving is something a little more personal. For example, you could have "Friends forever" or Thank you" or some other short sentiment inscribed. I, for one, would not be comfortable wearing a bracelet which had another man and woman's initials on it!

If a high-ranking official, such as a mayor, governor, or Supreme Court judge, will be performing the ceremony as a special favor to either of the families, he is not given a fee. A gift is sent to him later with a note of thanks by you and the groom. If someone such as a pastor or bishop performs the ceremony and if he receives a fee, it is up to you whether or not you send a small gift later with your thank you. If a friend of the family has the authority and is performing your ceremony, you will need to discuss payment with him if he customarily charges a fee. If he is not charging you, then you will definitely need to send a gift and thank you upon your return from your honeymoon. If he is charging a small fee, then you probably should send a little something along with your thank you as well.

You may wish to send a gift to both sets of parents as a very special thank you for one of the most memorable days of your life. It need not be expensive–just sentimental and lasting. Again, something engraved is always appropriate. You can wait and present it to them on your return or you can have it delivered the day following the wedding so they will know how much you appreciated all of their efforts.

You will want to give all of those special persons a special thank-you note, maybe one that is handmade so it is a gift in and of itself. If someone helped a little more than you asked or is very close to you, you may want to remember them with a small gift. Again it need not be expensive, just lasting and memorable. Participants you may want to thank are:

- Friends and relatives who host parties.

- Ceremony soloists or musical performers.

- Guest book attendant.

- Person in charge of wedding gifts at the reception.

- Servers.

- Friends or family who drive out-of-town guests before, during, and after the festivities.

- Baby-sitters.

- Friends who house or host wedding participants or guests.

I would maintain that thanks are the highest form of thought; and that gratitude is happiness doubled by words.

G.H. Chesterton

Index

Joy is the most infallible sign of the presence of God.

Leon Blox